LEARNING THE ROPES

Written by Nette Hilton
Illustrated by Lucia Masciullo

Published by Pearson Education Limited, Edinburgh Gate, Harlow, Essex, CM20 2JE
Registered company number: 872828

www.pearsonschools.co.uk

Text © Nette Hilton 2012

Designed by Bigtop
Original illustrations © Pearson Education Limited 2012
Illustrated by Lucia Masciullo

The right of Nette Hilton to be identified as author of this work has been asserted by her in
accordance with the Copyright, Designs and Patents Act 1988.

First published 2012

2022
13

British Library Cataloguing in Publication Data
A catalogue record for this book is available from the British Library

ISBN 978 0 435 07586 6

Printed and bound in Great Britain by Ashford Colour Press Ltd.

Acknowledgements
We would like to thank the children and teachers of Bangor Central Integrated Primary School,
NI; Bishop Henderson C of E Primary School, Somerset; Brookside Community Primary
School, Somerset; Cheddington Combined School, Buckinghamshire; Cofton Primary School,
Birmingham; Dair House Independent School, Buckinghamshire; Deal Parochial School, Kent;
Holy Trinity Catholic Primary School, Chipping Norton; Lawthorn Primary School, North
Ayrshire; Newbold Riverside Primary School, Rugby and Windmill Primary School, Oxford for
their invaluable help in the development and trialling of the Bug Club resources.

Every effort has been made to contact copyright holders of material reproduced in this book.
Any omissions will be rectified in subsequent printings if notice is given to the publisher.

CONTENTS

CHAPTER ONE

The Very Best Fun

It was that time of year again. The time I dreaded. The notice had gone up in school - our class was going on a Fun Camp.

Last year, when Oska Binns was my only best friend, we got out of going on the camp. We pretended we were ill. But Oska Binns moved house, and now he lives a long way away.

My new friend, who lives next door in Oska's old house, is Mitzi – and she said that a camp is the very, very, *very* best fun anyone could have.

"You should see the obstacle course, Spike!" she said. She calls me Spike even though my name is Max. "It's the best."

I asked my dad what an obstacle course was and he said it was something that made things harder to do.

"How can THAT be fun?" I asked Mitzi.

"You go over things instead of just running in a straight line!" she said. "It's great. There are rope ladders and big rope nets that hang from really high bars. And there are low benches that you have to crawl under. Sometimes there's mud, too. And a Flying Fox zip wire! Just wait till you see the Flying Fox, Spike! You'll never want to be in an ordinary race again."

WELCOME TO FUN CAMP!

LAKE

FLYING FOX

OBSTACLE COURSE

CAMPFIRE

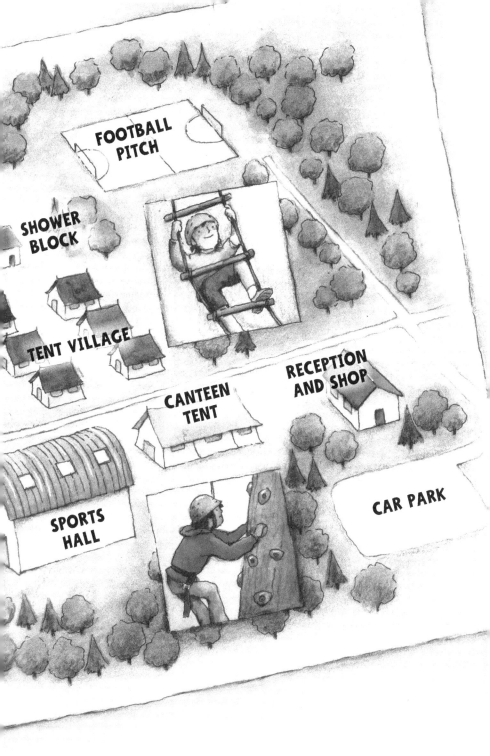

FOOTBALL PITCH

SHOWER BLOCK

TENT VILLAGE

CANTEEN TENT

RECEPTION AND SHOP

SPORTS HALL

CAR PARK

I'm not very good at races. I always come last. It was all right when Oska was with me. He would come last, too.

"Is there a beach?" I said. I'm better at swimming. I can swim all the way across the indoor pool near my house. Sometimes I can even do it without touching the bottom. My dad says it's best to try and keep going. He says, "You'll get there in the end, and that's all that matters."

"I hope not!" said Mitzi. "Climbing's more fun. And Flying Foxes. They're the best fun of all."

I think a camp is more fun if you stay away. Oska thought so, too.

CHAPTER TWO
The Secret

I felt sick on the bus. Mitzi said it wasn't
fair that we had to sit at the back, so she
made sure we were moved to the front.

"You don't get sick at the front," she
said.

I was glad Mitzi was with me. We were
going to be partners in everything. She
had put our names on all the lists.

We were going to rock-climb, run up the scramble net, play parachute games, fly down the Flying Fox, belly-roll through barrels and jump over mud puddles on the obstacle course. I felt sick all over again. There were so many things to do, and they all sounded very hard.

"You'll be all right, Spike!" Mitzi said when she set off for the girls' tents. "I'll be there to keep you going."

The boys' tents were very noisy.

Jamie and Ned were having a pillow fight, and Dan and Harry were planning tricks to play later on. Our team leader, Smithy, said everyone had to shush because we had to get our raft team ready.

"What sort of a raft?" Wills said.

"A raft that will float across the lake," said Smithy.

Some kids sat down. "Is it deep?"

"Not too deep," said Smithy. "You need to be able to swim, though. Can you all swim?"

"No," said the sitting-down kids.

"Yes," I said when it was my turn. "Sometimes I have to put my foot on the bottom, though."

"You'll be all right, then," said Smithy. "It's not that far, and you'll all have life-belts. And our raft won't sink anyway."

I hoped not. Lakes have ducks on them. I didn't want to fall in any water that had duck poo in it.

"Can girls be on our team?" I said.

"The girls have their own teams," Smithy said. "We have to beat them."

It'd be funny being on a team without Mitzi.

It'd be funny being on a team.

As long as Mitzi was out on the lake, too, it wouldn't matter. I would be all right.

"Remember not to tell anyone," Smithy said. "Our raft must be a secret!"

"How will it be a secret if everyone can see us building it?" Dan was looking around.

"It *has* to be a secret, though." Smithy was very firm. "We don't want anyone to know what our ideas are, do we?"

"No!" we all roared.

I didn't roar too loudly. I was still thinking about lakes and ducks.

And I was trying really hard to imagine how we might be able to put sides on our raft. That way, no one would fall overboard. Especially me.

I tried as hard as I could, but the only rafts I knew were the ones made with just a few boards tied together.

"Can rafts have seat belts?" I asked when it was my turn to share my idea.

Harry and Dan split their sides laughing, but Smithy said he didn't think so and it was a good idea just the same. It showed that I was on track!

"First, we'll draw up our plan, and then we'll get busy," Smithy was saying. "Don't worry about building it. I've got a secret place picked out. The most important thing, though, is ..."

"... IT'S A SECRET!"

CHAPTER THREE

Feet Up! Swing!

It was funny having a
secret that Mitzi didn't know.

I thought she might tell me that her
tent-team was building a raft for the race,
too, but when I found her the next day
she didn't say a word. There wasn't time.

We were all off for a run. It was our
morning warm-up. I think it should have
been called our morning hot-up. When we
finished, my face was so red that Mitzi
said I looked like a beetroot. Her face
was red, too, and I said she looked like a
tomato.

After breakfast, Mitzi grabbed me and put us in line for the Flying Fox.

It was awful.

Mitzi said the first thing I had to do was climb up a tree. I said the first thing I had to do was watch. I wanted to see what was going to happen.

Mitzi went first. "Watch me!" she called. I didn't take my eyes off her.

She climbed onto the little platform halfway up the tree. The Flying Fox leader was waiting.

"STRETCH UP!" he yelled.

Mitzi did. She held on to a bar above her head. The leader tied a harness around her middle. Then he stretched her towards him. She looked like a piece of elastic.

"READY?" the leader roared.

I wasn't sure if Mitzi *was* ready, but she was on her way anyway.

"FEET UP! SWING!"

Mitzi did. She swooshed over the mudpool and landed safely on the other side.

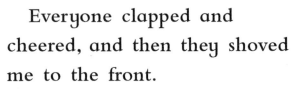

Everyone clapped and cheered, and then they shoved me to the front.

"Hurry up," they said. "Don't waste time."

I was there before I knew it. I think the leader might have helped. He leaned down and lifted me right up to the little platform.

"READY?" came the roar again.

I wasn't, but it didn't matter anyway. I was so frightened I couldn't close my eyes.

Over there, in the landing space, was grass and a little hill that was supposed to stop you. Some kids just kept going when it was their turn. Up and over.

Down there, before the landing place and right across the middle, was the biggest, yuckiest, slushiest mud puddle I'd ever seen.

"FEET UP! FEET UP! SWING!"

I tried. But it was too late.

My feet were down. They were jammed in place like rusty brakes on a bicycle. My toes dug in and I fell, face first, into the mud.

"Never mind, Spike," Mitzi said as we walked to the rope-jungle gym. "There's no mud here to fall into."

There was a very high bar, though. And big holes in the jungle gym for my feet to fall through.

At least there was a long line of kids waiting for their turn. I stood at the end for as long as I could.

CHAPTER FOUR

Anchor Man

I climbed the rope and didn't fall off.

We played a game with a parachute and I fell down three times. The third time the kids behind me didn't get tangled up.

The parachute leader said we'd get there in the end and I just had to remember to pick my feet up a bit more.

I picked them up as high as I could. Mitzi said I looked like a galloping horse.

Everyone wanted to be a galloping horse then. The parachute leader said I was really cool for thinking of it.

I said it was Mitzi's idea. She said I was the one who did it first and that made all the difference.

We didn't go to the rock wall to climb. We were getting ready, but Smithy said our team had to go back for a special meeting about you-know-what.

I looked for Mitzi to say we'd meet up later on, but she wasn't anywhere to be found. I asked her team leader if she knew where Mitzi was.

"No," she said. "She's in the other team now."

I didn't know what that
meant. I was going to ask,
but Smithy was waiting.

"HEY SPIKE!"
he yelled. "WE'RE
WAITING!"

I hurried over.
We were going on
a scavenger hunt. We
needed to find bits and
pieces that we could use to
build our raft.

"Keep up, Spike," said Smithy when
we set off. "We need you. You're our
anchor man!"

I wasn't sure what an anchor man
did. I did know that an anchor sits on
the bottom of the sea to keep the ship
from sailing away.

There was no way I wanted to sit on the bottom of a lake. But I did feel a little bit important being the anchor man, just the same.

Later, when we'd all finished planning and scavenging and showering and eating our tea in the canteen, I asked Mitzi if she knew what an anchor man did. She said she didn't know. She said she didn't care, either.

She had more important things on her mind, she said.

CHAPTER FIVE
Ready, Steady, Go!

It was Friday before we knew it. Race day. Mitzi had kept us busy practising for the obstacle race. Smithy had kept us busy, too.

As soon as we had finished our morning tasks, we had to line up.

"NOW LISTEN CAREFULLY!" yelled Mrs Jeffrey, the camp leader. "THE OBSTACLE COURSE IS OVER THERE."

We turned to look. It just looked like a lot of trees clumped together, and we could only see a little bit of track.

"DON'T WORRY. YOU WON'T GET LOST!"

I think she must have read my thoughts.

"THERE ARE LITTLE RED FLAGS TO SHOW YOU THE WAY! READY ..."

Mitzi grabbed me. "Run hard, Spike! We're going to win this one!"

Everyone had to be tied to their partner. We tied our bands around our wrists. Some kids tied them on their belts.

"STEADY ..."

We checked we were in the right
starting position.

"GO!" A whistle blew, and we were off.

A lot of kids stumbled and tripped over,
but we didn't. We were right up near the
front. I think Mitzi ran a bit faster than I
did. My feet didn't always get to touch the
ground.

We were going fast, fast, fast.

Then the kids in front of us fell over.
We were winning.

"Go!" called Mitzi. "Go Spike – go!"

I *was* going. It was ace!

And then ...

And then ... Mitzi stopped.

She stopped so suddenly that I slammed right into her back.

"What?" I cried.

She just shook her head. "Sorry, Spike."

CHAPTER SIX

Lean On Me

I ducked around Mitzi.

There was a log across a little stream. It wasn't a very wide stream and it had slippery banks that led down into the narrow stretch of water. It wasn't too far down. It wasn't too far from our side to the other, either.

It was too far to jump, though.

That was why the log was there. We had to run along it to get to the other side of the stream.

"Go on," I said. "Hurry up."

The others were starting to catch up. I could hear them crashing along behind us.

"We're done, Spike." Mitzi sat down. "There's no way I'm going over *that*."

"It's just a log," I said.

I could hear voices now, as the rest of the racers looked for the red flags.

"It's not the log," Mitzi said. "It's what's under it."

"Water?" I said.

"Water," she nodded. "I can't swim, Spike."

"But it won't be deep." I knew it
couldn't be. The camp leaders wouldn't
let kids who couldn't swim fall into deep
water. "Come on. Try."

Mitzi stood up. "Nope," she said. "It's
deep. I know it."

"It's just muddy," I said. "You can't see
the bottom, that's all."

Mitzi was already starting to go back
the way we'd come. I was still tied to her
wrist and was being dragged along behind
her.

We'd never win the race if we didn't
cross this stream.

I hauled Mitzi back. I grabbed her wrist
and pulled her to the log.

"Don't look down." I gave her a gentle push. She put one foot on the smooth bark. "It's only four or five steps. You'll be OK. I promise."

"There's no room for both of us!" She looked like she was going to step back.

"You go along the log and I'll go this way," I said as I held onto her hand and slowly, slowly started down the muddy bank to the water's edge.

"You'll get wet!" she howled. "You'll drown."

"No, I won't. I'll hold on to you," I promised.

Other kids were scrambling along the stream's edge looking for other logs.

I didn't hurry. "Lean on me if you feel you're going to fall."

Mitzi leaned on me really hard, but she kept going. Ducks quacked and scurried away. My shoes were sucked into the mud at the bottom of the stream but we managed to cross all the way over.

"Now RUN!" I said.

We ran so hard that my shirt stuck to my back.

But we didn't win.

"Never mind," said Mitzi. "We got there in the end."

Then I remembered the raft race was next and I felt a bit sick. I was still worried about being the anchor man.

CHAPTER SEVEN

Winners For Sure!

Smithy laughed when I asked him if I had to sit on the bottom of the lake.

"You sit at the back of the raft and hold them all steady," he told me when I asked how I was going to breathe down there. "You tell them what to do. They'll be counting on you. There's no way we'll let you fall in."

Even if they did, it wouldn't matter. I was already wet and muddy. And I can swim. A bit.

"I'm going to cheer hardest for you, Spike," said Mitzi. "I don't know what I would have done without you."

I grinned at her.

I do know I wouldn't have been anchor man or even have gone to camp without her. And I knew one other thing. As soon as the summer holidays came, I was going to teach Mitzi to swim.

Then watch out next year! We'll be the obstacle course race winners for sure!